Never Give In!

Sir Winston Spencer Churchill, 1874-1965

NEVER GIVE IN !

The Challenging Words of

Winston Churchill

With an Introductory Essay

by Dwight D. Eisenhower

Selected by

Dorothy Price and Dean Walley

Illustrated by Joe Isom

Hallmark Editions

CONTENTS

SIR WINSTON CHURCHILL:
A PERSONAL VIEW

by Dwight D. Eisenhower

On the eve of the Nazi invasion of Poland in September, 1939, Winston Churchill—his sixty-fifth birthday a little more than three months off—could look back on a long lifetime distinguished by more success in more careers than could most men of his age.

He had been a combat soldier on the Empire's far frontiers; a political leader not bound to partisan machines, for he had changed party affiliations when conviction so dictated; a principal architect of Britain's naval greatness in World War I; a strategist of that war whose daring plan, if it had been daringly executed, might have saved many millions of lives; a newspaper correspondent and author whose works in history and in biography had won him enduring fame.

In that season of 1939, his present was controversial and his future obscure: he was the prophet unheeded. Through the years, sometimes almost alone, his voice had been raised in warnings against Nazi aggression, in pleas that Britain prepare for war total beyond human experience. His warnings were soon fully to be realized, although his pleas had been inadequately answered.

Within a few weeks, however, he would return to the Admiralty and the office he had first assumed almost thirty years before. Nine months later, as Britain faced up to the darkest hours in its history, he became war leader of a beleaguered kingdom and its dominions beyond the sea.

Through three years of war, we were in constant association. So long as my headquarters were in England, preparing for the invasion of North Africa and, later, the liberation of the European continent, we met formally twice each week: for Tuesday lunch at 10 Downing Street; and for Friday evening discussions that often continued into the morning, either there or at Chequers, the Prime Minister's country place. On occasion we went together on extensive inspection tours among Allied troops.

But the man, at once so restlessly impatient at getting things done personally and so eager for information at first-hand, could not abide by any fixed schedule. Often, unheralded, he descended on me to present a new idea, to argue once again a rejected proposal, to get the latest word on battle—or just to chat.

Through my wartime association with him, the whole globe seemed to be an exercise ground for a mind that could, almost in the same instant, wrestle with an immediate problem in the deployment of air and land and sea forces and probe into the far-off future, examining the coming peacetime role of the embattled nations, shaping for his listener the destiny of the world.

Forever conscious of his responsibilities on the world scene and of his place in world history, Winston Churchill was, nevertheless, devoid of pompous stuffiness or of indifference to those about him. When Nazi planes swept up the Thames estuary on a raid over London, his habit was, when duty permitted, to search out his daughter Mary, a sergeant in an anti-aircraft battery, and assure himself of her safety. At other times, he would visit the burning districts, heartening and encouraging the homeless survivors of the raid. His siren suit on those occasions, that might well have made any other man a ridiculous figure, became a symbol of Londoners' ability to withstand the terror of fire bomb and blockbuster.

The immensity of his energy, of his devotion to a cause, of his scorn for those who despaired, and of his faith in Britain were daily manifest throughout the war. At all times he seemed to be Britain itself; by those around him and even by his deadliest enemies in the Axis camp he was so recognized. Seldom in history has one man so greatly symbolized a race of men and women, their strengths and their loyalties. But the stature of his leadership was not solely a creation of war.

When he had passed the biblical three score years and ten, rejected in his political leadership by the people he had led to victory, he moved against a new challenge. His party crushed, the aging Churchill took on the heavy task of rebuilding its ranks and restoring it to national power. The political saga of those years, quieter in tone and less dramatic in its movements and maneuvers, was as Churchillian in its tale of ultimate triumph as the saga of war. He became in 1951, once again, Britain's Prime Minister.

After I had been elected President, I was privileged to be associated with him in problems of world-wide scope, both of us still working in support of freedom and in opposition to all forms of tyranny. In personal conversation face to face and in many trans-Atlantic phone calls, I found him, despite the weight of years, still a source of inspiration, of wisdom, above all of faith that right and justice firmly maintained will ever triumph.

Half American by ancestry and citizen of all the free world by the leadership he gave it, Winston Churchill was the authentic Englishman all his days.

Neither England nor the world shall soon look upon his like again.

NEVER GIVE IN!

World War II:
Blood, Toil, Tears, and Sweat

As Prime Minister during the dark days of World War II, Winston Churchill delivered some of the world's most memorable speeches. The selections here show his unshakable confidence in the Allied cause, his remarkable understanding of international conflict, and his fierce will to win.

COME THEN: let us to the task, to the battle, to the toil—each to our part, each to our station. Fill the armies, rule the air, pour out the munitions, strangle the U-boats, sweep the mines, plough the land, build the ships, guard the streets, succour the wounded, uplift the downcast, and honour the brave. Let us go forward together in all parts of the Empire, in all parts of the island. There is not a week, nor a day, nor an hour to lose. *Manchester, January 27, 1940*

I WOULD SAY to the House, as I said to those who have joined this Government: "I have nothing to offer but blood, toil, tears, and sweat." We have before us an

3

ordeal of the most grievous kind. We have before us many, many long months of struggle and suffering. You ask: "What is our policy?"

I will say: "It is to wage war by sea, land, and air with all our might, and with all the strength that God can give us; to wage war against a monstrous tyranny, never surpassed in the dark lamentable catalogue of human crime." That is our policy. You ask: "What is our aim?"

I can answer in one word: "Victory!" Victory at all costs, victory in spite of all terror, victory however long and hard the road may be; for without victory there is no survival.

House of Commons, May 13, 1940

THIS IS one of the most awe-striking periods in the long history of France and Britain. It is also beyond doubt the most sublime.

Side by side, unaided except by their kith and kin in the great Dominions and by the wide Empires which rest beneath their shield—side by side, the British and French peoples have advanced to rescue not only Europe but mankind from the foulest and most soul-destroying tyranny which has ever darkened and stained the pages of history.

Behind them—behind us—behind the armies and fleets of Britain and France—gather a group of shattered States and bludgeoned races: the Czechs, the

4

Poles, the Norwegians, the Danes, the Dutch, the Belgians—upon all of whom the long night of barbarism will descend, unbroken even by a star of hope, unless we conquer, as conquer we must; as conquer we shall. *World Broadcast, May 19, 1940*

EVEN THOUGH large tracts of Europe and many old and famous States have fallen or may fall into the grip of the Gestapo and all the odious apparatus of the Nazi rule, we shall not flag or fail. We shall go on to the end. We shall fight in France, we shall fight in the seas and oceans, we shall fight with growing confidence and growing strength in the air; we shall defend our Island whatever the cost may be.

We shall fight on the beaches, we shall fight on the landing grounds, we shall fight in the fields and in the streets, we shall fight in the hills; we shall never surrender; and even if, which I do not for a moment believe, this Island or a large part of it were subjugated and starving, then our Empire beyond the seas, armed and guarded by the British Fleet, would carry on the struggle, until, in God's good time, the New World, with all its power and might, steps forth to the rescue and the liberation of the Old.

House of Commons, June 4, 1940

HITLER knows that he will have to break us in this Island or lose the war. If we can stand up to him, all

Europe may be free and the life of the world may move forward into broad, sunlit uplands. But if we fail, then the whole world, including the United States, including all that we have known and cared for, will sink into the abyss of a new dark age made more sinister, and perhaps more protracted, by the lights of perverted science.

Let us therefore brace ourselves to our duties, and so bear ourselves that, if the British Empire and its Commonwealth last for a thousand years, men will say, "This was their finest hour."

House of Commons, June 18, 1940

AND NOW it has come to us to stand alone in the breach, and face the worst that the tyrant's might and enmity can do . . . .

We are fighting *by* ourselves alone; but we are not fighting *for* ourselves alone. Here in this strong City of Refuge which enshrines the title-deeds of human progress and is of deep consequence to Christian civilization; here, girt about by the seas and oceans where the Navy reigns; shielded from above by the prowess and devotion of our airmen—we await undismayed the impending assault.

Perhaps it will come tonight. Perhaps it will come next week. Perhaps it will never come. We must show ourselves equally capable of meeting a sudden violent shock, or what is perhaps a harder test, a prolonged vigil. But be the ordeal sharp or long, or both, we shall seek no terms, we shall tolerate no parley; we may show mercy—we shall ask for none.

World Broadcast, July 14, 1940

I HAVE only one purpose, the destruction of Hitler, and my life is much simplified thereby. If Hitler invaded Hell I would make at least a favorable reference to the Devil in the House of Commons.

House of Commons, June, 1941

SOME DAY, when children ask "What did you do to win this inheritance for us, and to make our name so respected among men?" one will say: "I was a fighter pilot"; another will say: "I was in the Submarine Service"; another: "I marched with the Eighth Army"; a fourth will say: "None of you could have lived without the convoys and the merchant seamen"; and you in your turn will say, with equal pride and with equal right: "We cut the coal."

Speech to Coal Miners, October 31, 1942

THE GERMANS have received back again that measure of fire and steel which they have so often meted out to others . . . .

Now this is not the end. It is not even the beginning of the end. But it is, perhaps, the end of the beginning.

Mansion House, November 10, 1942

Mr. Churchill crossed the Rhine only two days after the Allied armies. As he later wrote, "I said to Montgomery, 'Why don't we go across and have a look at the other side?' Somewhat to my surprise he answered, 'Why not?' " from *The Second World War*

ONE DAY President Roosevelt told me that he was asking publicly for suggestions about what the war should be called. I said at once "the Unnecessary War." There never was a war more easy to stop than that which has just wrecked what was left of the world from the previous struggle.

from The Second World War

AT THE summit the stamina and valour of our fighter pilots remained unconquerable and supreme. Thus Britain was saved. Well might I say in the House of Commons: "Never in the field of human conflict was so much owed by so many to so few."

from The Second World War

IT IS A curious fact about the British Islanders, who hate drill and have not been invaded for nearly a thousand years, that as danger comes nearer and grows they become progressively less nervous; when it is imminent they are fierce, when it is mortal they are fearless. These habits have led them into some very narrow escapes.   from The Second World War

Message to General Eisenhower: I deem it highly important that we should shake hands with the Russians as far to the east as possible.   *April 2, 1945*

GOD BLESS you all. This is your victory! It is the victory of the cause of freedom in every land. In all our long history we have never seen a greater day than this. Everyone, man or woman, has done their best. Everyone has tried. Neither the long years, nor the dangers, nor the fierce attacks of the enemy, have in any way weakened the independent resolve of the British nation. GOD BLESS YOU ALL. May you long remain as citizens of a great and splendid city. May you long remain as the heart of the British Empire. *May 8, 1945*

THE ROAD across these five years was long, hard, and perilous. Those who perished upon it did not give their lives in vain. Those who marched forward to the end will always be proud to have trodden it with honour. from *The Second World War*

Hands Across the Sea:
England and America

Winston Churchill's mother was Jennie Jerome, a beautiful New Yorker. Mr. Churchill cherished a special fondness for Americans, as they did for him. "A son of America though a subject of Britain," he became, in 1963, at the age of 89, an honorary citizen of the United States by proclamation of President John F. Kennedy.

UNDOUBTEDLY these two great organizations of the English-speaking democracies—the British Empire and the United States—will have to be somewhat mixed up together in some of their affairs for mutual and general advantage. For my own part, looking out upon the future, I do not view the process with any misgivings. I could not stop it if I wished—no one can stop it. Like the Mississippi, it just keeps rolling along. Let it roll! Let it roll on in full flood, inexorable, irresistible, benignant, to broader lands and better days. *House of Commons, August 20, 1940*

THE BRITISH people are good all through. You can test them as you would put a bucket into the sea, and always find it salt. The genius of our people springs from every class and from every part of the

12

land. You cannot tell where you will not find a wonder. The hero, the fighter, the poet, the master of science, the organizer, the artist, the engineer, the administrator, or the jurist—he may spring into fame. Equal opportunity for all, under free institutions and equal laws—there is the banner for which we will do battle against all rubber-stamp bureaucracies or dictatorships.   *Radio Broadcast, June 13, 1945*

THE AMERICAN eagle sits on his perch, a large, strong bird with formidable beak and claws. There he sits motionless and M. Gromyko [Soviet delegate to the U.N.] is sent day after day to prod him with a sharp pointed stick—now his neck, now under his wings, now his tail feathers. All the time the eagle keeps quite still. But it would be a great mistake to suppose that nothing is going on inside the breast of the eagle.   *House of Commons, July 5, 1946*

THERE ARE no people in the world who are so slow to develop hostile feelings against a foreign country as the Americans and there are no people who, once estranged, are more difficult to win back.

THE AMERICANS took but little when they emigrated from Europe except what they stood up in and what they had in their souls. They came through, they tamed the wilderness, they became "a refuge for the oppressed from every land and clime." They have become today the greatest State and power in the world, speaking our language, cherishing our common law, and possessing, like our great Dominions, in broad principle, the same ideals.

House of Commons, October 28, 1947

I AM A child of the House of Commons. I was brought up in my father's house to believe in democracy. "Trust the people," was his message.... In my country, as in yours, public men are proud to be servants of the State and would be ashamed to be its masters.

United States Congress, December, 1941

HE [Franklin Roosevelt] was the greatest American friend that Britain ever found, and the foremost champion of freedom and justice who has ever stretched strong hands across the oceans to rescue Europe and Asia from tyranny and destruction. I will go further and place on record my conviction that in his life and by his action he changed, he altered, decisively and permanently the social axis, the moral axis of mankind by involving the New World inexorably and irrevocably in the fortunes of the Old. *London, April 12, 1948*

A MAJOR difference between the state of the world after the First and after the Second World Wars is that the United States, instead of retiring into isolation, instead of demanding full and prompt payment of debts and disinteresting herself in Europe, has come forward step by step and has made the great counter-poise upon which the freedom and the future of our civilization depends.

House of Commons, November 30, 1950

LET ME tell you what General Eisenhower has meant to us. In him we have had a man who set the unity of the Allied Armies above all nationalistic thoughts. In his headquarters unity and strategy were the only reigning spirits. The unity reached such a point that British and American troops could be mixed in the line of battle and large masses could be transferred from one command to the other without the slightest difficulty.

At no time has the principle of alliance between noble races been carried and maintained at so high a pitch. In the name of the British Empire and Commonwealth I express to you our admiration of the firm, far-sighted, and illuminating character and qualities of General of the Army Eisenhower.

from *The Second World War*

FOR AT LEAST two generations we were, as the American writer Walter Lippman has reminded us, a guardian, and almost a guarantor of the Monroe Doctrine . . . . We and the civilized world owe many blessings to the United States, but have also in later generations made our contribution to their security and splendor. *Westminster, May 7, 1946*

THE BRITISH and Americans do not war with races or governments as such. Tyranny, external or internal, is our foe, whatever trappings or disguises it wears, whatever language it speaks or perverts.

I HAVE never accepted a position of subservience to the United States. They have welcomed me as the champion of the British point of view. They are a fair-minded people. *Woodford Green, October 10, 1951*

BRITAIN and the United States are working together, and working for the same high cause. Bismarck once said that the supreme fact of the nineteenth century was that Britain and the United States spoke the same language. Let us make sure that the supreme fact of the twentieth century is that they tread the same path.   *United States Congress, January 17, 1952*

AMONG Englishmen I have a special qualification for such an occasion; I am directly descended through my mother from an officer who served in Washington's Army. And as such I have been made a member of your strictly selected Society of the Cincinnati. I have my pedigree supported by affidavits at every stage . . . .

The drawing together in fraternal association of the British and American people, and of all the people of the English-speaking world, may well be regarded as the best of the few good things that have happened to us and to the world in this century of tragedy and storm.

Independence Day Dinner, London, July 4, 1950

YOU [America] may be larger and we [Britain] may be the older. You may be the stronger, sometimes we may be the wiser.

WE MUST be very careful nowadays—I perhaps all the more because of my American forebears—in what we say about the American Constitution. I will therefore content myself with the observation that no Constitution was ever written in better English.

Westminster Hall, May 27, 1953

LET US stick to our heroes John Bull and Uncle Sam.

Mansion House, November 9, 1953

Let Us Learn our Lessons:
Wisdom of a Great Leader

Perhaps more than any other man of this century, Winston Churchill experienced the tragedy of long, hard-fought wars which failed to bring lasting peace. His military career spanned cavalry and bomber warfare. From his personal experiences come these still timely observations.

MIGHT not a bomb no bigger than an orange be found to possess a secret power . . . to blast a township at a stroke . . . guided automatically in flying machines by wireless or other rays, without a human pilot?

1925

Animal Disarmament

ONCE upon a time, all the animals in the zoos decided that they would disarm, and they arranged to have a conference to arrange the matter. So the Rhinoceros said, when he opened the proceedings, that the use of teeth was barbarous and horrible and ought to be strictly prohibited by general consent. Horns, which were mainly defensive weapons, would, of course, have to be allowed.

The Buffalo, the Stag, the Porcupine, and even the little Hedgehog, all said they would vote with the

Rhino. But the Lion and Tiger took a different view. They defended teeth, and even claws, which they described as honorable weapons of immortal antiquity. The Panther, the Leopard, the Puma and the whole tribe of small cats all supported the Lion and the Tiger.

Then the Bear spoke. He proposed that both teeth and horns should be banned and never used again for fighting by any animal. It would be quite enough

if animals were allowed to give each other a good hug when they quarreled. No one could object to that. It was so fraternal and that would be a great step toward peace. However, all the other animals were very offended with the Bear, and the Turkey fell into a panic.

The discussion got so hot and angry that all those animals began thinking so much about horns and teeth and hugging when they argued about the peaceful intentions that had brought them together, that they began to look at one another in a very nasty way. Luckily, the keepers were able to calm them to go back quietly to their cages and they began to feel quite friendly with one another again.   *October, 1928*

NOTHING is more dangerous in war-time than to live in the temperamental atmosphere of a Gallup Poll, always feeling one's pulse and taking one's temperature. I see [it said that] leaders should keep their ears to the ground. All I can say is that the British nation will find it very hard to look up to the leaders who are detected in that somewhat ungainly posture.

House of Commons, September, 1941

LET US learn our lessons. Never, never, never believe any war will be smooth and easy, or that anyone who embarks on the strange voyage can measure the tides and hurricanes he will encounter. The statesman who yields to war fever must realize that, once the signal is given, he is no longer the master of policy but the slave of unforeseeable and uncontrollable events.   *News Report, January, 1942*

To HEAR some people talk one would think that the way to win a war is to make sure that every power contributing armed forces and branches of these armed forces is represented on all the councils and organizations which have to be set up, and that everybody is fully consulted before anything is done. That is, in fact, the most sure way to lose a war.

House of Commons, January 27, 1942

WAR IS very cruel. It goes on for so long.

THE DARK AGES may return—the Stone Age may return on the gleaming wings of science; and what might now shower immeasurable material blessings upon mankind may even bring its total destruction. Beware, I say! Time may be short.

From Stettin, in the Baltic, to Trieste, in the Adriatic, an iron curtain has descended across the Continent. Behind that line lie all the capitals of the ancient States of Central and Eastern Europe—Warsaw, Berlin, Prague, Vienna, Budapest, Belgrade, Bucharest, and Sofia. All these famous cities and the populations around them lie in the Soviet sphere, and all are subject in one form or another not only to Soviet influence, but to a very high and increasing measure of control from Moscow. Athens alone, with its immortal glories, is free to decide its future at an election under British, American, and French observation. *Fulton, Missouri, March 5, 1946*

LET there be sunshine on both sides of the iron curtain; and if ever the sunshine should be equal on both sides, the curtain will be no more.

Blenheim, August 4, 1947

LITTLE did we guess that what has been called "The Century of the Common Man" would witness as its outstanding feature more common men killing each other with greater facilities than any other five centuries put together in the history of the world.

Massachusetts, March 31, 1949

WHEN I was a schoolboy, I was not good at arithmetic, but I have since heard it said that certain mathematical quantities when they pass through infinity, change their signs from plus to minus—or the other way around . . . . This rule may have a novel application, and that when the advance of destructive weapons enables everyone to kill everybody else, nobody will want to kill anyone at all.

House of Commons, November 3, 1953

Commenting on the Cold War: What we are faced with is not a violent jerk but a prolonged pull.

IT MAY be that we shall by a process of sublime irony have reached a stage in this story where safety will be the sturdy child of terror, and survival the twin brother of annihilation.   *News Report, March 3, 1955*

GREAT wars come when both sides believe they are more or less equal, when each thinks it has a good chance of victory.

WARS are not won by evacuations.

TWICE in a single generation the catastrophe of world war has fallen upon us; twice in our lifetime has the long arm of Fate reached across the ocean to bring the United States into the forefront of the battle. If we had kept together after the last war, if we had taken common measures for our safety, this renewal of the curse need never have fallen upon us.

Do we not owe it to ourselves, to our children, to mankind tormented, to make sure that these catastrophes shall not engulf us for the third time?

from *The Second World War*

I Shall Have no Misgivings:
Personal Reflections

Through all his long years, Winston Churchill actively pursued life. He lived always by his own standards rather than those of a fickle world. "The only guide to a man is his conscience," he writes in this sampling of his personal attitudes.

I HAVE been a journalist and half my lifetime I have earned my living by selling words and, I hope, thoughts.

WE CANNOT say "the past is past" without surrendering the future.

THE TRUTH is incontrovertible. Panic may resent it; ignorance may deride it; malice may destroy it, but there it is. *House of Commons, May 17, 1915*

MORAL force is, unhappily, no substitute for armed force, but it is a very great reinforcement.
House of Commons, December 21, 1937

THE ONLY guide to a man is his conscience; the only shield to his memory is the rectitude and sincerity of his actions. It is very imprudent to walk through life without this shield, because we are so often mocked by the failure of our hopes; but with this shield, however the Fates may play, we march always in the ranks of honour.

House of Commons, November 12, 1940

I DRAW a distinction between mistakes. There is the mistake which comes through daring—what I call a mistake toward the enemy—in which you must sustain your commanders . . . . There are mistakes from the safety-first principle—mistakes of turning away from the enemy; and they require a far more acid consideration. *House of Commons, May 7, 1941*

THERE IS only one answer to defeat, and that is victory. *House of Commons, June 10, 1941*

THE PROBLEMS of victory are more agreeable than those of defeat, but they are no less difficult.

House of Commons, November, 1942

THE HUMAN story does not always unfold like a mathematical calculation on the principle that two and two make four. Sometimes in life they make five or minus three; and sometimes the blackboard topples down in the middle of the sum and leaves the class in disorder and the pedagogue with a black eye.

London, May 7, 1946

I AM surprised that in my later life I should have become so experienced in taking [honorary] degrees when as a schoolboy I was so bad at passing examinations. In fact, one might almost say that no one ever passed so few examinations and received so many degrees. From this a superficial thinker might argue that the way to get the most degrees is to fail in the most examinations . . . .

No boy or girl should ever be disheartened by lack of success in their youth but should diligently and faithfully continue to persevere and make up for lost time.   *Miami, Florida, February 26, 1946*

IF YOU have a motor-car . . . you have to have a brake. There ought to be a brake. A brake, in its essence, is one-sided; it prevents an accident through going too fast. It was not intended to prevent accidents through going too slow. For that you must look elsewhere . . . . You must look to the engine and of course to the petrol supply. For that there is the renewed impulse of the people's will; but it is by the force of the engine, occasionally regulated by the brake, that the steady progress of the nation and of society is maintained.　　　　*House of Commons, November 11, 1947*

It would be a great reform in politics if wisdom could be made to spread as easily and as rapidly as folly.

It takes too poor a view of man's mission here on earth to suppose that he is not capable of rising—to his material betterment—far above his day-to-day surroundings . . . . The dominant forces in human history have come from the perception of great truths and the faithful pursuance of great causes.

There is no doubt that it is around the family and the home that all the greatest virtues, the most dominating virtues of human society, are created, strengthened, and maintained.

On the birth of Prince Charles, November 16, 1948

Twenty to twenty-five! These are the years! Don't be content with things as they are. "The earth is yours and the fulness thereof." Enter upon your inheritance, accept your responsibilities. Raise the glorious flags again, advance them upon the new enemies, who constantly gather upon the front of the human army, and have only to be assaulted to be overthrown.

Don't take "No" for an answer. Never submit to failure. Do not be fobbed off with mere personal success or acceptance. You will make all kinds of mistakes; but as long as you are generous and true, and also fierce, you cannot hurt the world or even seriously distress her. She was made to be wooed and won by youth. She has lived and thrived only by repeated subjugations. from *My Early Life*

AT BLENHEIM I took two very important decisions: to be born and to marry. I am happily content with the decisions I took on both occasions.

DON'T give your son money. As far as you can afford it give him horses. No one ever came to grief— except honourable grief—through riding horses. No hour of life is lost that is spent in the saddle. Young men have often been ruined through owning horses, or through backing horses, but never through riding them; unless of course they break their necks, which taken at a gallop, is a very good death to die.

from *My Early Life*

NEVER give in! Never give in! Never, Never, Never, Never—in nothing great or small, large or petty— never give in except to convictions of honour and good sense. *Speech at the Harrow School*

BY A blessed dispensation, human beings forget physical pain much more quickly than they do their joyous emotions and experiences. A merciful Provi-

dence passes the sponge of oblivion across much that is suffered, and enables us to cherish the great moments of life and honour which come to us in the march.   *House of Commons, October 21, 1949*

MAN IN this moment of history has emerged in greater supremacy over the forces of nature than has ever been dreamed of before . . . . There lies before him, if he wishes, a golden age of peace and progress. All is in his hand. He has only to conquer his last and worst enemy—himself.

House of Commons, March 28, 1950

I HAVE never had the advantage of a university education. But it is a great privilege and the more widely extended, the better for any country. It should not be looked upon as something to end with youth but as a key to open many doors of thought and knowledge. A university education ought to be a guide to the reading of a lifetime . . . .

One who has profited from university education has a wide choice. He need never be idle or bored. He is free from that vice of the modern age which requires something new not only every day but every two or three hours of the day . . . . The first duty of a university is to teach wisdom, not a trade; character, not technicalities. We want a lot of engineers in the modern world, but we do not want a world of engineers.

House of Commons, September 19, 1950

NATURALLY I am biased in favor of boys learning English. I would make them all learn English: and then I would let the clever ones learn Latin as an honour, and Greek as a treat. But the only thing I would whip them for is not knowing English. I would whip them hard for that.   from *My Early Life*

SCIENCE, which now offers us a golden age with one hand, offers at the same time with the other the doom of all that we have built up inch by inch since the Stone Age and the dawn of any human annals. My faith is in the high progressive destiny of man. I do not believe we are to be flung back into abysmal darkness by those fiercesome discoveries which human genius has made. Let us make sure that they are servants, but not our masters.

Plymouth, October 23, 1951

YOU REMEMBER Fulton. [Where Mr. Churchill delivered his famous "Iron Curtain" address.] I got into great trouble being a bit in front of the weather that time. But it's all come out since—I won't say right, but it's all come out.

Aboard the Queen Mary, January, 1953

On receiving the Nobel Prize for Literature: I am proud, but also, I must admit, awestruck at your decision to include me. I do hope you are right. I feel we are both running a considerable risk and that I do not deserve it. But I shall have no misgivings if you have none.

Read by Lady Churchill in Oslo, December 10, 1953

CHANGE is the master key. A man can wear out a particular part of his mind by continually using it and tiring it, just the same way as he can wear out the elbows of a coat by rubbing the sleeves or shoulders: but the tired parts of the mind can be rested and strengthened not merely by rest, but by using other parts . . . . Many men have found great advantage in practicing a handicraft for pleasure. Joinery, chemistry, bookbinding, even bricklaying —if one were interested in them and skillful at them—would give relief to the overtired brain.

from *Painting as a Pastime*

EXPERT knowledge, however indispensable, is no substitute for a generous and comprehending outlook upon the human story, with all its sadness and with all its unquenchable hope.

My MOTHER made a brilliant impression upon my childhood's life. She shone for me like the evening star—I loved her dearly, but at a distance.

Eels Get Used to Skinning:
The Churchill Wit

Although knighted in 1954, Great Britain's most famous citizen preferred the plain "Mr. Churchill" to the courtly "Sir Winston." He seldom failed to see a situation's humor. His unassuming manner endeared him to the common people he called his own.

THIS interlude of school makes a somber grey patch upon the chart of my journey. I am all for the Public Schools, but I do not want to go there again.

from *My Early Life*

WHEN I was a young subaltern in the South African War, the water was not fit to drink. To make it palatable, we had to add whiskey. By diligent effort, I learned to like it.

I NEITHER want it [brandy] nor need it but I should think it pretty hazardous to interfere with the ineradicable habit of a lifetime.

ALL I can say is that I have taken more out of alcohol than alcohol has taken out of me.

WHEN I warned the French that Britain would fight

on alone whatever they did, their generals told their Prime Minister and his divided cabinet, "In three weeks England will have her neck wrung like a chicken." Some chicken. Some neck.

Ottawa, December 30, 1941

POLITICS are almost as exciting as war, and quite as dangerous. In war, you can only be killed once, but in politics many times.

ALTHOUGH always prepared for martyrdom, I preferred that it should be postponed.

To the United States Congress: I cannot help reflecting that if my father had been an American and my mother British, instead of the other way round, I might have got here on my own.   *December 16, 1941*

Lady Astor reportedly once told Mr. Churchill that if she were his wife, she would poison his coffee. Mr. Churchill retorted, "If you were my wife I'd drink it."

A FANATIC is one who can't change his mind and won't change the subject.

WHAT most people call bad judgment is judgment which is different from theirs at a particular moment.

On Charles de Gaulle: We all have our crosses to bear. Mine is the Cross of Lorraine.

SOME people's idea of free speech is that they are free to say what they like, but if anyone says anything back, that is an outrage.

When Mr. Churchill was wearing a moustache, as a young man, he once took a young lady to dinner who held opposing political opinions. "Mr. Churchill," she said, "I care for neither your politics nor your moustache." He answered, "Don't distress yourself. You are not likely to come in contact with either."

IT IS hard, if not impossible, to snub a beautiful woman — they remain beautiful and the rebuke recoils.

I AM reminded of the remark of the witty Irishman who said: "There are a terrible lot of lies going about the world, and the worst of it is, that half of them are true."

MY VARIOUS readings led me to ask myself questions about religion. Hitherto I had dutifully accepted everything I had been told. I had always had to go to church once a week. All this was very good. I accumulated in those years so fine a surplus in the Bank of Observance that I have been drawing confidently upon it ever since.

WELL, one can always consult a man and ask him, "Would you like your head cut off tomorrow?" and after he has said, "I would rather not," cut it off. "Consultation" is a vague and elastic term.

House of Commons, May 7, 1947

40

When Mr. Churchill was defeated in the elections of 1945, Lady Churchill told him, "It may well be a blessing in disguise." He replied, "At the moment, it seems quite effectively disguised."

FOR MY part, I consider that it will be found much better by all parties to leave the past to history, especially as I propose to write that history myself.

House of Commons, January 23, 1948.

THERE is a good saying to the effect that when a new book appears one should read an old one. As an author I would not recommend too strict an adherence to this saying.   *Oslo, May 12, 1948*

JUST as eels get used to skinning, politicians get used to being caricatured.

THE word "disinflation" has been coined in order to avoid the unpopular term "deflation." I suppose that presently when "disinflation" also wins its bad name, the Chancellor will call it "non-undisinflation" and will start again.

House of Commons, October 27, 1949

SHORT words are best and the old words when short are best of all.

WRITING a book was an adventure. To begin with it was a toy, an amusement; then it became a mistress, and then a master, and then a tyrant.

London, November 2, 1949

DURING my life I have often had to eat my own words and I have found them a wholesome diet.

On the occasion of his seventy-fifth birthday: I am ready to meet my Maker. Whether my Maker is prepared for the great ordeal of meeting me is another matter.

November 30, 1949

IT IS a very fine thing to refuse an invitation, but it is a good thing to wait till you get it first.

43

I HOPE you have all mastered the official Socialist jargon which our masters, as they call themselves, wish us to learn. You must not use the word "poor"; they are described as the "lower income group." When it comes to a question of freezing a workman's wages the Chancellor of the Exchequer speaks of "arresting increases in personal income."

There is a lovely one about houses and homes. They are in the future to be called "Accommodation Units." I don't know how we are to sing our old song "Home, Sweet Home." "Accommodation Unit, Sweet Accommodation Unit, there's no place like our Accommodation Unit." I hope to see the British democracy spit all this rubbish from their lips.

Cardiff, February 8, 1950

I CAN practice, in an honorary fashion, the arts of surgery and medicine. Unless there is a very marked shortage of capable men in both these professions, I will not press myself upon you. No doubt in these difficult times it will be a comfort not only to the profession but to the nation at large that you have in reserve. I have not yet taken any final decision as to which of those beneficent branches I should give priority in case an emergency arises. Being temperamentally inclined to precision and a sharp edge, it might be thought that I should choose the surgeon's role. *London, July 10, 1951*

44